HOW THINGS WORK

MONSTER
MACHINES

p

This is a Parragon Publishing Book
This edition published in 2001

Parragon Publishing
Queen Street House
4 Queen Street
Bath BA1 1HE, UK

Copyright © Parragon 2000

ISBN 0-75255-299-6

Printed in Dubai, U.A.E

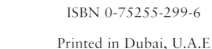

Produced by
Monkey Puzzle Media Ltd
Gissing's Farm
Fressingfield
Suffolk IP21 5SH
UK

Illustrations: Alex Pang, Cara Kong,
Adrian Wright and Studio Liddell
Designer: Tim Mayer
Cover design: David West Children's Books
Editor: Linda Sonntag
Editorial assistance: Lynda Lines and Jenny Siklós
Indexer: Caroline Hamilton
Project manager: Katie Orchard

Photos supplied by MPM Images

Contents

BUCKETWHEEL EXCAVATOR

Unloading
When the bucket reaches the top of the wheel, it tips its load onto a moving conveyor belt.

Cables
Strong steel cables are used to raise and lower the bucketwheel.

Bucketwheel
The wheel has large buckets attached to its rim—large enough to hold a small family car. As the wheel turns, the buckets dig into the coal. The wheel can dig out 40,000 buckets of coal in a day.

Bucket

Operator's cabin
The operator has to adjust the speed, height, and position of the bucketwheel. He must also avoid large rocks that could damage the machine. In fact, it takes five workers to run the excavator. One operates the excavator, while the other four watch from near by, keeping in contact with the operator on a two-way radio.

Strip mine
A large mine, such as the copper strip mine at Bingham Canyon, near Salt Lake City, Utah, can produce 265,680 tons of ore in a day. The deepest strip mine in the world is near Bergheim, Germany. It is 1,066ft (325m) deep.

MONSTER MINING MACHINE

The gigantic bucketwheel excavator is a powerful machine used in strip mining, where the coal is just under the surface of the ground. First the soil on top of the coal is scraped away. Then the excavator digs the coal with its huge buckets, which turn on a revolving belt. It dumps the coal onto a conveyor belt that carries it off to be stored, or to waiting railroad trucks. Bucketwheel excavators are also used in quarries to mine minerals and metal ores. For these jobs, the machine is fitted with a crusher. First the rock is blasted, then the excavator scoops it up, crushes it, and feeds it onto the conveyor belts.

Built on site
The excavator is so large it has to be built on-site. This can take up to 2 months.

Boom
The boom, or frame, supports the wheel and conveyor belt.

Engines
Powerful diesel engines are needed to turn the bucketwheel.

Crusher
The huge lumps of coal or ore may pass through a crusher inside the machine. This grinds them to a size that's easier to handle.

Conveyor belt
A conveyor belt carries the coal to a railroad siding where it is dumped into a railroad truck. Some coal may be piled up in a storage area.

Crawler tracks
The excavator moves on huge crawler tracks. Each track is larger than a semi. This machine has 16 tracks.

GUIDED BY LASER

It may be a monster machine, but the bucketwheel excavator is also a precision instrument that uses the very latest laser technology. A laser beam guides the excavator on its path so that its buckets cut into the coal face at exactly the right place and to the right depth. If the excavator is not in exactly the right place, it will dig out rock and soil as well as coal, making the operation less efficient and more expensive. The bucketwheel excavator was one of the first industrial machines to be equipped with a laser.

CONCRETE MIXER TRUCK

Drum
Just before the truck arrives at the construction site, the driver pumps water into the drum. The drum turns about 12 times a minute to mix the concrete.

Hopper
Sand, cement dust, and crushed rock are loaded into the drum through the hopper.

Mixing blades
Welded inside the drum are spiral-shaped blades called flights. These push the concrete to the front or back of the drum, depending on which way the drum is turning.

Unloading
To unload the concrete, the driver changes the direction of the drum. The concrete pours out of the drum onto the delivery chute.

Delivery chute
Concrete pours down the delivery chute to the concrete pump.

Delivery pipe
The concrete is pumped through a pipe on the outside of the boom. The pipe is made in sections that pass through the boom at the joints. This allows the pipe and boom to be folded for storage.

Swivel
This turns to point the boom in the correct direction so that the concrete goes where it is needed.

POURING CONCRETE
Concrete is pumped to the upper stories of a tall building. The hopper delivering the concrete can move to allow the concrete to be spread wherever it is needed.

MIXING CONCRETE

Concrete is used to build tall blocks of offices and apartments cheaply and quickly. It is a wet mixture of sand, cement, crushed rock, and water that sets hard as it dries. When an office block is being built, wet concrete is poured into a steel framework, where it dries to form the floors and walls of the building. Concrete is made and delivered to the building site in a concrete mixer truck. The truck has a large revolving drum to hold the dry ingredients and the driver pumps in water just before the truck reaches the site. The drum turns all the time to keep the concrete well-mixed and to keep it from setting. The truck holds about 15 tons of concrete. It is over 24ft (7m) long and weighs just under 6 tons when unloaded.

Water tank
This holds water used to make the concrete and to wash the drum after discharging the concrete.

Driver's cab
The driver operates the mixer controls from the cab.

Outrigger
The outriggers, or stabilizers, extend to help keep the truck steady when the boom is extended. Without outriggers, the truck could tip over.

Two engines
Some mixer trucks have two engines, one to turn the mixing drum and another to drive the truck. Other mixers have only one engine to perform both tasks.

Levers
Levers control the operation of the drum.

PUMPING CONCRETE

The mixer truck arrives at the construction site and the driver unloads the concrete by reversing the direction of the mixing drum. The concrete flows down the delivery chute into a concrete pump. A piston in the pump forces the wet concrete through a long pipe and into the building. The machine has to be extremely powerful to pump concrete into the upper stories. Workers smooth the concrete over the floor, or channel it into hollow casings to form the walls. When the concrete sets hard, the casing is removed.

EARTHSCRAPER

Quick-release mechanism
This releases the windows in an emergency.

Steering mechanism
Hydraulic rams use the pressure of oil to generate the large force needed to turn the wheels.

Scraper control
This raises and lowers the cutting edge.

Exhaust pipe
The fumes produced by the engine are carried away by the exhaust pipe.

Driver's cabin
An earthscraper is difficult to drive because it has two separate engines to control. Also, the long body is articulated—it can bend in the middle.

Front engine
The front engine is a powerful four-stroke diesel engine with 16 cylinders, like a large truck engine.

Automatic transmission
The transmission automatically adjusts the amount of power fed to the wheels from the engine. Less power is needed in loose soils than in hard, compacted soils.

Powerful brakes
The earthscraper has powerful brakes. These work by pressing a pad called a brake shoe against a drum attached to each wheel.

SMOOTHING THE GROUND

An earthscraper is a huge machine used to level and smooth out large areas of ground. This machine is 49ft (15m) long and 11ft (3.4m) wide. It weighs 86 tons—as much as 60 family cars. Road construction teams use earthscrapers to cut through low hills so that a new road can be laid. The machine stores the soil it scrapes away. It can either dump it in one place to build up an embankment, or release it gradually, spreading it over the ground to fill in small pockets in the ground.

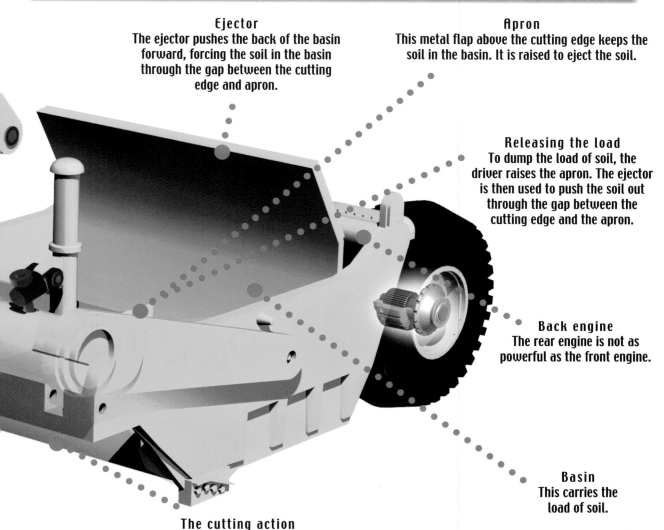

Ejector
The ejector pushes the back of the basin forward, forcing the soil in the basin through the gap between the cutting edge and apron.

Apron
This metal flap above the cutting edge keeps the soil in the basin. It is raised to eject the soil.

Releasing the load
To dump the load of soil, the driver raises the apron. The ejector is then used to push the soil out through the gap between the cutting edge and the apron.

Back engine
The rear engine is not as powerful as the front engine.

Basin
This carries the load of soil.

The cutting action
The cutting edge cuts 12in (300mm) into the ground. After it is lowered, the cutter slices easily through the ground—the soil curls up like butter on a knife. The soil moves into the basin where it is stored until dumping.

WORKING IN PAIRS

An earthscraper has two engines. One powers the front of the machine, where the driver sits, and the other powers the back, where the scraper cutting edge is. Two earthscrapers are often teamed up so a job can be done twice as fast. Double earthscrapers often get stuck in soft ground. A bulldozer has to push them out. The back of the scraper is specially strengthened to handle the force of the bulldozer.

POWER SHOVEL

Small shovel
This power shovel is a small one. It is only 43ft (13m) long and weighs just under 6 tons.

Boom

Open and shut
This ram uses oil pressure to transmit the force of a piston to the bucket bottom. This system, called a hydraulic ram, opens and closes the bucket.

Up and down
This hydraulic ram raises and lowers the boom.

Bucket
The bucket is hinged in the middle so it can open to drop a load. Some very big mining shovels have eight buckets attached to a large wheel that revolves as the machine cuts into the coal.

Replaceable teeth
The teeth on the bucket are designed to sharpen themselves as they cut into the coal. They can be replaced when they eventually wear out.

Headlight
Powerful headlights shine on the coal for working at night.

Swing motor
The swing table is turned by an electric or hydraulic motor. This swings the boom around for unloading.

Bucket hinge
The bucket opens and shuts here.

COMPUTER CONTROLS

Monster machines like the power shovel need to be carefully controlled, or they could do a lot of damage. If they are overloaded or break down they are extremely expensive to repair. So the power shovel has built-in computer systems that automatically shut down the engine if there is the danger of being overloaded. Sensors around the shovel monitor engine performance, temperature, and oil pressure. The computer gives a warning if the engine is not operating correctly.

Exhaust pipe
This carries away the waste gases and fumes produced by the engine.

Air filter
This filters out the dust in the air, making sure that only clean air goes to the engine.

Engines
The shovel has two powerful diesel engines. If one engine breaks down, the other takes over.

Driver's cab
The cab is 18ft (6m) from the ground. It is both soundproof and vibrationproof. The operator pulls levers to move the boom, and to open and close the bucket.

Oil tank
This holds the oil for the hydraulic systems.

Crawler tracks
These are driven by the diesel engine. The shovel can move around safely on the soft soil found in strip mines. The tracks work separately—to turn the shovel, one track is driven forward while the other is driven backward or kept still.

Swing table
The cab and boom rest on a circular table that can be turned to swing the upper part of the machine around.

BIG DIGGER

A power shovel digs coal out of the walls of an coal strip mine. This monster machine has a huge bucket at the end of a long arm, or boom—it carries up to 1,507cu ft (140cu m) of coal. The boom stretches up the mine to scrape out coal with the bucket. When the bucket is full, the driver swings the arm around and dumps the coal onto a waiting semi. A power shovel works fast—it can fill a large semi with 118 tons of coal in just two minutes. Power shovels are driven by gasoline or diesel engines, or by electric motors.

The Marion 6360 power shovel has a boom length of 220ft (67m) and a reach of 236ft (72m). It weighs 1,082 tons, and uses 20 electric motors to power the boom and bucket. It works in a strip mine near Percy, Illinois.

TOWER CRANE

ANCHOR

The tower is anchored to large concrete blocks or set into a concrete base. Above 200ft (60m), a tower crane is often linked to the building it is working on for extra stability.

Lifting winch
This winch winds in the hoist cables to lift the load. The rope is wound around a drum. The winch is powered by an electric motor.

Trolley winch
This winch winds in the cables attached to the trolley to move it along the main jib.

Counterweight jib
This long arm, or jib, carries the counterweights.

Driver's cab
The driver sits in a cab and controls the winches that move the trolley along the arm and lift the load. A worker on the ground guides the driver using a walkie-talkie radio. An alarm system in the cab warns the driver if a load is too heavy to lift.

Counterweights
These heavy concrete blocks balance the crane and keep it from falling over as it lifts a load.

Tower
The tower is made up of steel sections bolted together. Each section is 20ft (6m) tall.

Ladder
The driver may have to climb over 100 steps to reach the cab.

Tower cranes are built piece by piece on the construction site. They get slowly taller as more sections are added to the tower. A small mobile crane places the first few sections of the tower in place. After that, a special section, called a climbing frame, is added. The crane lifts a new section and places it inside the climbing frame. A hydraulic ram, a lifting device at the base of the climbing frame, pushes the new section up. The climbing frame is then raised and the whole process is repeated again.

Cantilever cables
These support the jibs and allow heavier weights to be lifted. The crane can lift the heaviest weight when the trolley is near the tower. The strain on the jib is greatest when the trolley is at the end of the main jib.

Trolley cables
These cables control the movement of the trolley.

Trolley
The trolley moves back and forth along the jib on wheels. It is pulled along by cables attached to the trolley winch. The load hangs below the trolley.

Main jib
The jib can usually swing around in a complete circle.

Hoist, or lifting, cables
These cables lift the load.

Lifting hook

Turning around
The crane can swing around in a complete circle on a revolving plate. The plate is turned by an electric motor.

BUILDING SKYSCRAPERS

Tower cranes are the tallest cranes in the world. They are used to help build tall buildings like skyscrapers. They lift things to the top of the building under construction. A tower crane has a long horizontal arm, called a jib, which turns on top of a tall tower. The jib carries a movable trolley, from which the load hangs on steel cables. Electric motors connected to winches wind in the cables attached to the load and trolley. The cables pass around pulleys, which reduce the force needed to lift the load. However, using pulleys increases the length of cable that has to be wound in.

PAPERMAKING MACHINE

SPECIAL PAPER
Small papermaking machines are used to make special or high-quality paper. This is used in expensive books and presentation scrolls.

Support mesh
Wire mesh supports the wet layer of pulp while the water drains and is sucked out. The web is then strong enough to be lifted off the mesh of wire.

Keeping watch
Workers can walk around the walkway at the top of the machine to keep watch and make repairs.

Felt belt
The felt belt carries the wet web to the press rollers.

Pulp mixture
It takes 12 trees to make about 1 ton of paper.

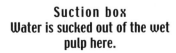

Suction box
Water is sucked out of the wet pulp here.

Press rollers
These rollers squeeze more water out of the web.

CHINESE PAPER
The Chinese discovered how to make paper about 2,000 years ago. They boiled old fish nets and rags with water, and then beat them to make a soft, wet pulp. A mesh made of fine crisscrossed wires was dipped into the pulp and then removed with a layer of pulp on it. After the water had drained away, the layer of pulp was pressed and dried to make paper.

FROM TREE TO PULP

Today, papermaking is basically the same as it was 2,000 years ago, except that the raw material is wood from trees such as pine and spruce. They are grown in plantations for the paper industry. The papermaking machine was invented in 1803 by two English brothers, Henry and Sealy Fourdrinier. Papermaking machines are sometimes called Fourdrinier machines. First, the bark is stripped from the wood, then the wood is ground to a pulp by giant grinders. The pulp is cooked with chemicals to break it into fibers. Then it is washed, bleached, and beaten to produce smaller, finer fibers. Finally, it is mixed with water and fed into the papermaking machine.

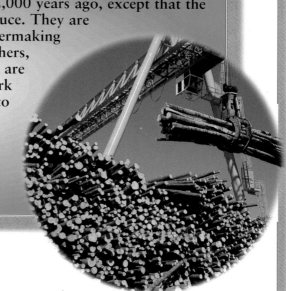

Calender rollers
The calender rollers smooth the surface of the paper.

Heated drying rollers
The heated drying rollers take water out of the paper in the form of steam.

Long machine
Papermaking machines are over 650ft (200m) long and can produce more than 295 tons of paper in a day. Over 3,280ft (1,000m) of paper races through the machine every minute.

Jumbo
The paper is wound on a large reel called a jumbo. It can be attached and removed without stopping the machine.

Computer control panels
A computer checks the strength, thickness, and color of the paper. Only a few people are needed to look after the huge machine.

MAKING PAPER

In a papermaking machine, the wet pulp is spread on a wire mesh that turns on rollers. The mesh vibrates and the water drains out of the pulp, leaving a smooth layer of fibers, called the web. The web passes onto a moving belt made of felt. Then it goes through a series of rollers called press rollers, which squeeze out more water. The web then passes between heated drying cylinders, which remove the remaining water. Finally, the web passes through an upright stack of rollers, called the calender, which smooth its surface.

PRINTING PRESS

Inking rollers
There are different kinds of inking roller. Some have a rubber surface, others have a metal surface. They make sure that ink is spread evenly over the plate.

Ink trough
Each of the four presses has a trough that holds the ink.

Printing press 2
prints magenta (red).

Printing press 4
prints black.

Printing press 1
prints cyan (blue).

Printing press 3
prints yellow.

Printing plate
The printing plate holds the image to be printed. Ink is spread over the image so that it transfers onto the blanket roller.

Reel of paper
In an automated press, the reel can be changed without stopping the press.

Blanket roller
The rubber-coated blanket roller transfers the image from the plate to the paper. Its rubber surface prints evenly on the bumpy surface of the paper.

Transfer roller
The transfer roller carries the paper to the next printing plate. Mechanical grippers on the transfer drum hold the paper accurately in place so that the four colors are printed in register (in the correct place).

Paper web
The web, a continuous strip of paper, is fed through the press.

LETTERPRESS
Johann Gutenberg, a German goldsmith, invented printing using movable type in 1439. Individual letters were carved into small wooden blocks—the type. The blocks were placed in a frame, wiped with ink, and pressed onto paper to produce the printed page. This process is called letterpress printing. It is still used today, although offset lithography, shown here, is now much more common.

PRINTING SHEETS

Small printing presses print sheets of paper. Sheet-fed machines are used for printing books that require good-quality printing, unlike the machines used by many magazines and newspapers which are not intended to be kept for long.

LITHOGRAPHY

In lithography, a thin metal sheet called a plate, or stereo, is used to print pages. An image of the text and pictures to be printed is formed photographically on the plate. The plate is treated with chemicals to make ink stick to the dark parts of the image. The plate is often wrapped around a cylinder which rotates at high speed. As the cylinder rotates, the plate is pressed against paper coming off a large reel. The ink transfers to the paper, forming the printed image. In a similar process called offset lithography, the image is first transferred to a rubber cylinder, called the blanket roller, which then prints onto paper.

Dryer
Heated plates dry the ink on the paper, so that it is ready for folding.

Folder
The folding unit folds the printed magazines and papers.

Cut and stitch
The printed and folded pages are cut to the correct size. Then they are stapled or stitched together in sections.

Fast workers
Printing presses can produce 60,000 copies of a color magazine in one hour.

PRINTING A PICTURE

Printed pictures are produced using a pattern of small dots of ink. There are many dots where the picture is dark and fewer where the picture is light. This allows the light and dark shades of the picture to be reproduced. To print a full-color picture, four separate plates are made. One plate prints the cyan (blue) parts of the picture. Other plates print the magenta (red), yellow, and black parts. All the colors in a picture can be reproduced using only these four colors.

THE LONDON EYE

Inside an egg

The 32 fully-enclosed, egg-shaped passenger cars, or capsules, each weigh about 9 tons and hold 25 people. The capsules are attached to the outer rim, and each one has an individual motor to rotate it as the wheel goes around. They are heated in the winter and air-conditioned in the summer.

Round and round

One circuit of the wheel takes half an hour.

By the river

The London Eye is located on the south bank of the Thames River in London, England. Although built to last 50 years, the wheel only has planning permission for five years. After that, Londoners will have to decide whether or not they want to keep it.

MONSTER TOURIST ATTRACTION

The London Eye was built as a tourist attraction to bring people to London for the Millennium celebrations. The 1,475-ton structure is heavier than 250 double-decker buses.

At night, the London Eye pulses gently with soft light—at 16 pulses a minute—our natural rate of breathing.

Foundations

The London Eye is built on 45 concrete piles sunk 108ft (33m) deep, containing 2,560 tons of concrete.

THE BIGGEST WHEEL IN THE WORLD

Imagine a bicycle wheel 120ft (36m) taller than Big Ben in London, and a third higher than the Statue of Liberty. Now you have some idea of the world's largest observation wheel. Towering 450ft (135m) over London, the London Eye is the city's fourth-tallest structure. It carries a total of 800 people in 32 observation cars on a 30-minute trip. From the top, the passengers can see up to 25mi (40km) in any direction, depending, of course, on the weather.

Stormy weather
The London Eye is designed to withstand the force of any possible storm. It has devices called mass dampeners, which are used in tall buildings, to keep it from swaying too much in strong winds.

Spokes
The main spokes are steel cables as thick as a person's arm. They weigh a total of 49 tons.

A-frame
The wheel is held on by a single support shaped like an "A," which is 216ft (66m) high.

Heave ho!
The London Eye is turned by electric motors and a diesel generator. If the motors fail, two people can turn the wheel by pulling it around with a piece of rope.

MORE GIANT WHEELS
The first big wheel was built in 1893 in Chicago, Illinois. It was called a Ferris wheel after its builder, George Ferris. It was 250ft (76m) in diameter and carried 2,160 passengers in 36 cars. One famous modern-day big wheel is also a clock! The Cosmoclock 21 in Yokohama City, Japan, is a Ferris wheel 344ft (105m) tall. It carries 480 passengers. Each of the 60 arms holding the observation cars acts as a second hand of a gigantic clock.

FLIGHT SIMULATOR

Instructor's console

Computer
The computer makes sure that the simulator moves like a real aircraft in response to the trainee pilot's actions. It also records a training session, so that the instructor and trainee pilot can learn from it afterward.

Instructor's console
The instructor sits at a console behind the trainee pilot. The console displays information about the pilot's performance. The instructor can tell the computer to simulate special conditions, such as foggy weather, or to give the trainee a difficult task, such as an emergency landing.

Pistons
The pistons tilt and roll the simulator to follow the pilot's commands. If the pilot pulls up on the joystick, the simulator tilts up to show that the airplane would tilt up. The pistons can also create the effect of air turbulence by making the simulator vibrate up and down.

LEARNING TO FLY
Trainee pilots can learn to fly an airplane without leaving the ground. They are trained on a computer-controlled flight simulator. This is a copy of a real cabin in which the trainee pilot sits. The simulator has all the control buttons and instruments found in a real airplane cockpit, and the pilot "flies" the simulator exactly as if it were the real thing. The computer makes the simulator react like an airplane—it tilts and rolls as the pilot moves the controls, and the instruments give realistic readings of such things as height and the amount of fuel left in the tanks. The simulator even reproduces the engine noise and the sound of air flowing past the airplane.

Projectors
Three projectors display a high-quality picture onto the curved screen. The computer generates the picture according to the pilot's commands. If a pilot is training to fly from a specific airport, that airport and the surrounding land are shown during the take-off and landing.

Screen
The screen stretches around the simulator so that the pilot has a view through the side windows as well as the front.

Curved mirror
The pilot views the pictures on the screen through a mirror that curves around the simulator. This set up gives the pilot a wide-angle view around the cabin and is very realistic.

Trainee pilot's display panel

Controls

Trainee pilot's seat

Fluid machines
The pistons are hydraulic machines. They are moved up and down by the pressure in a hydraulic fluid. They are controlled by the main computer and respond to the trainee pilot's actions.

LOOKING OUT
The computer creates realistic views in the simulator's cabin windows. Projectors under computer control throw pictures onto a screen. The pictures show what the pilot will see through the cabin window during a real flight. When the pilot is taking off or landing, the screen shows the airport runway just as it would be in real life. If there is danger of colliding with another airplane, the screen shows the other plane approaching fast!

ROLLER COASTER

Gravity

Most roller coasters are powered by gravity. The cars are pulled to the top of a steep slope and let go. Gravity pulls them down the slope, gathering enough speed to climb the next hill.

Gaining weight

As the car moves up a slope or twist, you appear to gain weight because inertia presses you into the seat. Inertia is the tendency of things to stay still unless they are forced to move.

Losing weight

As the car moves down a slope, you appear to lose weight.

Power cables

Some roller coasters are powered by electricity. There is an electric cable between the two rails.

MOMENTUM

When a roller coaster suddenly dives down, your stomach seems to get "left behind." This is because anything moving tends to keep going in one direction. This tendency is called momentum. If you were not strapped into your seat, momentum would continue to carry you uphill, and you would be thrown into the air as the car hurtled down.

Centrifugal force
At the top of a loop, you are pressed up into your seat by centrifugal force.

On rails
The wheels of a roller coaster fit in grooves in the rails. Because of this, the car can't leave the rails at the top of a steep drop.

Getting heavier
Turning the loop at the bottom of a valley, you feel a lot heavier. This happens because you are pressed down by the centrifugal force.

THRILLS WITHOUT SPILLS

Would you pay good money to be held upside-down screaming for your life? Yes—if the money bought you a ride on a roller coaster. These thrill rides with their cars speeding around crazy twists and loops, hurtling up dizzy heights and plummeting down heart-stopping drops appear dangerous, but are in fact perfectly safe—as long as the riders obey the rules. You can't fall out even when you're hanging upside-down at the top of a loop. The laws of science keep you glued in your seat.

The force that anchors you in your seat is called centrifugal force. This force acts whenever a moving object turns a corner. When you are in a car, centrifugal force pushes you to one side as the car goes around a corner. On the corkscrew section of a roller coaster, the car is constantly turning a corner. The centrifugal force presses the riders into their seats—even when they're upside-down!

HIGHEST, FASTEST, LONGEST

The highest and fastest roller coaster in the world is called *Superman—The Escape*. It is at Six Flags Magic Mountain in Valencia, California. The cars reach a speed of 100mph (161kph). The structure is 1,650 feet (503m) tall. The longest roller coaster in the world is at Lightwater Valley Theme Park in Ripon, England. Called *The Ultimate*, the ride is almost 2mi (3km) long.

OIL RIG

PLUMBING THE DEPTHS

The world consumes over 68 million barrels of oil a day. Much of it comes from large oil rigs, or platforms, scattered across the oceans of the world. These rigs either float on the sea or stand on the seabed. They drill into the seabed to the oil deposits beneath it. The oil is pumped to the surface and carried by tanker or pipeline to refineries on land. Natural gas is often found with the oil and can be extracted at the same time.

Gas purification system
The natural gas that comes to the surface with the crude oil is a mixture of gases. The useful part of the mixture is taken out, turned into a liquid, and sent ashore.

BRANCHING OUT

A system called directional drilling allows wells to be drilled at different angles instead of straight down. This means that many oil fields can be reached from one rig. A single rig can receive oil from up to 60 wells.

Rig support legs
The legs house the drill that digs its way down to the oil field. Once a well has been drilled, the legs contain the pipes carrying oil, gas, and water. The oil and gas are separated and purified. The gas is pumped to the mainland through pipes. When the pipeline is shut down, the gas is burned, or flared, off.

KINDS OF RIGS

A floating rig, or semi-submersible platform, rests on huge floats called pontoons. It is held in place above the oil well by steel cables that anchor each corner of the platform to the seabed. Some rigs, called guyed tower platforms, stand on a steel framework that reaches down to the seabed. The tower is anchored to the seabed with steel cables. Gravity platforms are the biggest and heaviest. These huge concrete structures rest directly on the seabed, held in place by their sheer weight. A platform is like a small town. It has its own power supply, water supply, living quarters, helicopter pad, and medical facilities. Oil workers may live and work on the rigs for weeks at a time.

The tallest oil rig is the *Mars* platform in the Gulf of Mexico. It rises 2,940ft (896m) from the seabed to the surface. It stands twice as high as the Empire State Building. The *Mars* platform produces 38,000 barrels of oil per day.

Flare
Excess gas, which comes up along with the oil, is burned off here.

Derrick
The derrick is used to hold lengths of pipe while the well is being drilled. When the well is producing oil, the derrick is used to repair the pipes connecting the well to the rig.

Crane
A crane is used to move objects around the rig, and to lower and raise diving bells.

Helicopter pad
Workers and supplies are flown to the rig by helicopter.

Living quarters
Workers may live on the rig for weeks at a time.

Oil purification system
Oil pumped from the well contains mud and sea water which have to be removed before the oil is taken to the onshore refinery.

Storage/ballast tanks
The base of a gravity rig consists of huge concrete tanks, each 66ft (20m) in diameter and 164ft (50m) high. These are used to store oil before it is collected by a tanker or pumped through a pipeline to the refinery on shore. The tanks are filled with sea water when there is no oil in them. The steel skirt around the bottom of the tanks cuts into the seabed, anchoring it there as the rig settles.

Oil!
An oil deposit may be 1.86mi (3km) below the seabed.

WIND TURBINE

WIND FARMS

A wind farm is a collection of wind turbines built on a high ridge, sea coast, or open plain. There may be hundreds of wind turbines in a wind farm. The largest wind farms generate as much electricity as three power stations. There are around 20,000 wind turbines producing electricity in the world today.

Gearbox
A gearbox links the turbine blades to the electricity generator. The gearbox ensures that the generator turns at a high speed whatever the wind speed. When the wind is weak and turns the turbine blades slowly, the gearbox increases the speed of the generator.

Control system
The control system automatically adjusts the direction and angle of the blades. This is important because the maximum amount of power must be extracted from the wind.

Generator
The generator produces electricity. Inside the generator a coil of wire turns near a magnet. An electric current is produced in the coil.

Cables
Underground cables carry the electricity to where it is needed.

POWER FROM THE WIND
For over 5,000 years, the wind has been used as a source of power. Windmills grind corn. Modern versions of the windmill generate electricity. These wind turbines, as they are called, have huge blades to catch the slightest wind. The blades are connected to an electricity generator. When the blades are turned by the wind, this turns the generator and produces electricity.

Motor
An electric motor automatically turns the turbine into the wind. The electric motor is like a generator in reverse—an electric current flows through a coil of wire near a magnet, and the coil is forced to rotate.

Sensors
The wind turbine is equipped with sensors that detect the wind speed and direction.

Nacelle
The nacelle, or outer covering, protects the machinery from the weather.

Positioning gear
This moves the turbine around so that its blades are always facing into the wind.

Tower
The tower contains the electricity cables and a ladder. It is tall enough to lift the turbine above the ground to catch the wind, and keeps the spinning blades a safe distance from the ground.

Blades
The blades are shaped like aircraft wings. The angle at which the blades are set can be changed to fit the wind speed and direction.

LARGEST WIND GENERATOR

The world's largest wind generator is in Oahu, Hawaii. The Trade Winds blow for most of the year there, making it a perfect spot for a wind generator. The wind turbine has two blades measuring 318ft (97m) from tip to tip, on a steel tower as tall as a 20-story building. The winds are so strong that the tower bends as the winds blow. The wind turbine generates enough power for 1,000 homes.

INDUSTRIAL ROBOT

Electricity cables

Sensor
Robot arms contain sensors that detect where the arm is and feed this information into the computer control unit. The computer checks that the arm is in the correct position. If not, the computer activates the motors to move the arm.

Computer unit
The computer holds the program that guides the robot arm. It receives information from the arm sensors and controls the motors that move the arm.

Robot hand
Car assembly robots can be equipped with many different kinds of tools—welding units, nozzles for spraying paint, sanding discs for smoothing surfaces, and electromagnets for lifting metal parts.

CARMAKING ROBOTS
Most of the world's robots are used to make cars. Each robot performs a single task on the car chassis as it moves along the production line.

HARD WORKERS
The popular idea of a robot is a machine that looks and acts like a human. But most robots are industrial robots, and don't look like us at all. The industrial robot is a computer-controlled mechanical arm. Robot arms can bend in every direction. At the end of the arm is the robot "hand." This is a tool such as a welder, paint sprayer, or gripper for grasping objects. These robots work around the clock in factories, doing jobs like welding metal parts together and painting the finished products. They live up to their name, since the word "robot" comes from the Czech word for a slave.

Welding metal
Welding is a process that joins pieces of metal together. The edges of the metal pieces are melted so that they flow together. Welding robots use a strong electric current to melt the metals.

ROBOT EYES
Some robots are fitted with vision units, or "eyes," to increase their usefulness. A welding robot without vision must have the parts it is welding placed in exactly the right position. But a robot with vision can check the position of the parts and adjust its actions accordingly.

Robot arm
The arm has shoulder, elbow, and wrist joints that can move in any direction.

Power unit
A robot arm is moved by electric motors, or by liquid pressure (hydraulics). Electric motors are used in the joints that rotate. Hydraulic power is used in joints that move up and down.

TEACHING A ROBOT
An industrial robot has to be programmed like a computer, to tell it what to do. There are two main ways of instructing industrial robots. The first is to work out exactly what movements are needed to complete a task, and to write these movements into a program for the control computer. The second is to teach the robot a job such as painting, by guiding its arm through the movements needed to complete the task. The robot is programmed to remember what it has been taught, and will repeat the movements exactly.

SPACE STATION

full view of Space Station

Communications antenna
Radio messages are sent to and from the Space Station using dishlike radio antennas. These antennas are highly directional and can pick up very faint signals.

Zarya Module

Docking port
The Space Shuttle and other craft can link up to the station at the docking port.

Living quarters
The living quarters in this module include a bathroom, sleeping quarters, and a gym with an exercise bike.

Unity Module

Science laboratory
This is where the astronauts will carry out experiments and astronomical observations.

Escape capsule
This will carry the astronauts back to Earth in an emergency.

BUILDING THE SPACE STATION

The world's most exciting space project, the International Space Station, is currently being built 217mi (350km) in orbit above the Earth. Assembly of the Space Station began in December 1998 and will be completed in 2004. The Space Station will be a gigantic 354ft (108m) across and 148ft (88m) long. It will weigh over 423 tons. It will take 45 shuttle launches to carry the construction parts of the station into orbit.

NASA will carry out most of the construction work and provide most of the modules that make up the station. Russia, Europe, Japan, Canada, and Brazil will also take part in the building and operation of the station.

Central framework

Solar panels
These provide the Space Station with power from the Sun. Two huge panels of solar cells, each the size of a football field, convert sunlight into electricity.

Robot arm
This is used to grasp and repair satellites. It is controlled by an astronaut inside the Space Station. Video cameras on the arm let the astronaut see what the arm is doing.

Payload servicing module
This module will have a pressurized workshop where the crew will repair and service satellites.

LIVING AND WORKING IN SPACE

The station will have modules for astronauts to live and work in. The modules will be attached to a long spine of inter-connecting beams called a truss. Huge solar panels will supply the station with electricity.

Up to seven astronauts will spend up to three months at a time working in the station. They will carry out all kinds of experiments and observations in orbit. The almost complete absence of gravity on the Space Station will allow experiments that are impossible on Earth. The station will also be used for recovering and repairing weather and communications satellites.

Index